The Moon Child

Padmini Govender

ISBN 978-1-0370-5540-9(print)

978-1-0370-5541-6(e-book)

Printed in the Republic of South Africa.
Copyright © Padmini Govender 2025

All rights reserved. No part of this book may be reproduced in any form or by any electronic or mechanical means, including information storage and retrieval systems, without written permission from the author, except in the case of a reviewer, who may quote brief passages embodied in critical articles or in a review. Trademarked names appear throughout this book. Rather than use a trademark symbol with every occurrence of a trademarked name, names are used in an editorial fashion, with no intention of infringement of the respective owner's trademark. The information in this book is distributed on an "as is" basis, without warranty. Although every precaution has been taken in the preparation of this work, neither the author nor the publisher shall have any liability to any person or entity with respect to any loss or damage caused or alleged to be caused directly or indirectly by the information contained in this book.

"Padmini's poetry emerges as a soul-stirring testament to the depth of the human spirit and the transformative power of spiritual self-realization. Her words are not merely poetic expressions but profound reflections of the universal truths that bind us all together. Through her mastery of language, wordsmith Padmini, invites readers on a journey of inner discovery, unravelling the layers of the self with eloquent elegance and humane spiritual insights. Her poetry is a testament to a Sacred Journey of the Divine and the Personal.

Her exploration of the Divine Feminine in poetry is deeply resonant. Padmini's words recognize the immense strength and resilience of women who, despite enduring societal oppression, continue to rise and forge their paths forward. The delicate balance between vulnerability and power, beauty and struggle, forms the foundation of her call to honour the Divine Feminine – the anima - within all beings. Her writings become an invitation to celebrate this sacred energy, not only within women but in all who embrace it.

Padmini's work is not just poetry; it is a sacred, timeless call to reclaim one's true essence and embrace the power of spiritual awakening. Through her lyrical mastery and deep spiritual insight, she opens pathways to healing, growth, and self-liberation. Her poetry is an invitation for us all, to journey through the depths of our being and return, to the Light of our Divine purpose."

-*Review by Mohamed Faruk Hoosain (MA UKZN)*

A collection of lotuses,
You may call me Roshnee,
I am light.

I am an earth child,
Don't ever cage me in,
Behind closed walls
Or through closed minds.

A little over a decade,
I sought healing for my body,
Healed my soul in the process,
And found my tribe.

In recent times, my thoughts
Become words that trail
Across paper and screen.

Dedication

To an angel daughter, Ekta Somera – *"Join the Literary group, Aunty Rosh,"* back in September 2022. *I am not sorry about that invitation.*

To my children, Revashni and Kevashan – *my very own cheerleaders, without them even knowing it. Some children are here to teach adults how to become better versions of themselves. We cannot remain stuck because we are afraid of change.*

To my husband, Sydney (from teenage love to a whole marriage) – *I have only shared this personal goal of publishing a book very recently.* "But you always wrote very well, from back in school."

The Universe knew that without Earth Angels to keep me focused, my writing would have only ever flown on the wings of the clouds.

Contents

Dark Moon   7

New Moon   77

Full Moon   143

Dark Moon

When the night is dark,
and the moon seems afraid
of its own emptiness,
where even the stars fade away,
that is when true shadow work begins.
For the moon can hide, but the truth cannot.

Divine Feminine

There are women who have
walked through burning coals
to raise their families and communities,
who deserve the accolades that may
or may not be bestowed on them.
There are women who are still lost,
trying to find their place in a society
often shunned and discarded.

A patriarchal world dictating
how women should be,
yet complaining when she's not
standing tall on her own strength.

There is no middle line, no safe space.
The best a woman can do is embrace
her feminine energy and forge ahead.
It often comes at a price.
Her light is dimmed with one fell swoop,
for this feminine energy
threatens the manhood of society.

Still, we must continue,
for it is only with the Divine Feminine
that we can bring this crazy world back to order.

The Crone Age

I am not a haggard, ugly witch to be banished from sight.
I seem difficult, even demanding, to those around me.
Why am I changing?
Why am I expecting to be understood?

After years of social conditioning, in various roles,
my soul is driven to break free from the shackles
of opinions and expectations that no longer serve me.
My soul cries out for me to honour myself.

I am not a wild horse that needs to be reined in,
but a woman who has served faithfully
and now needs to see to me.

The Fire

The fire pit with hot, cooled coals,
the mind steadfast in its purpose,
to focus with faith and walk
across the once red-hot embers.
Firewalking – a test of one's devotion.

The lessons the soul agreed to
come at one, hard and fast.
There is no solitude to prepare.
The fire rages, spitting and hissing.
One can succumb to the fiery pits of hell,
past pains and fear swallowing
one whole for more to come,
or one can slay the dragons,
one by one; each win pushes upwards,
while the fire burns out to ash.

Winter

I am told that winter
is a necessary inconvenience to every soul.
Hibernate, restore, rejuvenate,
revel in the rest and respite winter brings!
Every season has its purpose; it is how we balance life out.
My soul does not winter very well;
it dies a little, my heart saddens.
My emotions go everywhere,
and I become easily misunderstood.
As spring sneaks in, my soul starts feeling alive.
The tiniest bud, the birds flying in such hearty buoyancy,
the sun, warm and comforting,
the breeze, a kiss from the heavens.
If only every day were a summer day,
and if only all I needed to shift my energy
were warm days and blue skies.
Alas, winter is only three seasons away!
And comes with its own challenges for a sunbird like me.

Unwell Mind

Easily misunderstood,
it must be the moon.
I need medication,
it helps, I am told.

I am told what to think,
how to feel and act.
Think positive thoughts,
you will feel happy.
Stop that act of being sad.

My soul screams in pain,
with or without medication.
I am not much of the person
I am supposed to be.
Can this just end?

Crashing

I feel the rage, crashing harder each time,
seething up like a serpent uncoiling itself.
At a point, I become afraid of even myself,
knowing that I could make your life a living hell,
where you would beg death to come.
I have burned at the stake before;
that does not make my heart afraid.
It terrifies me that you choose to play
these childish games with me,
for when my patience runs dry,
and I no longer feel human,
nothing will save you
from the pain that will follow.

End of the Road

When you come to the end,
and there is not much road left,
the body wracked with pain,
the mind saying, "Go on,
be strong, you can beat this."
The heart says to think about
your wife, your parents, your family.

Your soul is saying, "No,
this is the end."
A body riddled with pain,
withered to the bone,
can no longer be home
to a beautiful soul.

I pray that the moment comes
in waves of love and light,
that your soul sees your waiting tribe,
and that you traverse in light.
It is only love that awaits us on the other side.

Villain

The emotions are wilding,
dragging me down.
Seems nobody understands.

My heart is racing
from the fear of wanting to
succumb to the depths of the ocean.

A tiny part of me is gasping for breath.
The rage that is burning my soul
will bring the village to ash.

I cannot still my thoughts, nor numb the pain.
Family thinks this is a game,
playing the victim, making me the villain.

Empty Soul

Your smile, so sweet and demure,
your voice and words so flowery,
such a beautiful soul,
caring and kind.

Innocence portrayed,
innocence taken astray.

That smile and those words
remain fixed on the lips only.
Eyes dead, no sparkle or shine,
empty words, cold and uncaring.
The mask you wear
fails to hide your empty soul.

Deceit

The sheer flamboyancy
and the grandeur of life,
the glitter and sparkle,
magnetic like a moth to a flame,
hypnotic and mesmerizing.
Careful camouflage of reality,
hiding away the treachery and deceit
behind the beautiful façade.

Fragments of Life

Nothing is whole nor perfect,
yet many are willing to die on that hill,
displaying model marriages,
luxurious lives, passports stamped full
of travel everywhere.
Not a stray hair out of place,
flawless makeup and haute couture.

When night creeps in, they fall apart,
broken and fragmented; alone and scared.
Going to sleep in mansions,
but no lover to hold tight,
tears messing up the satin sheets,
dreams ripping the fable into shreds.

It is easier to pick up the pieces of a soul
that recognises its flaws
than to fix up broken facades,
hiding behind the screens of perfection.

Live Feeds

Live feeds from every random soul,
opinions from faceless strangers,
love and heartbreak,
sordid details of messy breakups,
splashed all over,
strewn across public platforms.

Trendy, so fashionable,
enticing you to want the same.

People competing to be the best
or the worst they can ever be.
Every breath, captured on camera,
digitised for immortality.

When did we stop living?
When did living become acting?

Karma

Carefully and intricately designed,
Mangled words of hate,
Poisoned by deceit and lies,
Held together by threads of toxicity,
Invisible and unseen,
Or a web of golden yarn,
Glittering in the sun.
In the end, the web of the evil mind
Will entrap and drown the self,
For the soul cannot escape
The atrocities inflicted on another.

The Flow

There's a natural order of things.
When disrespected, it brings chaos.

It is not about individual egos,
but a collective that is destroyed.
It is not about me holding power
over you, or you being the winner.

It is about the natural order
of things that give rise to
a flow that brings harmony, peace, and love.

Times of Change

There was a time
when man and nature existed,
independent, yet interdependent.
When the sun and moon spoke to all,
unwritten rules convened
the way things should be,
before the times of change.

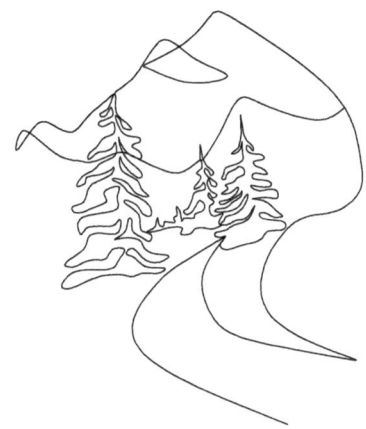

The Mist

The lone figure in the mist,
lost in the beauty of the sunrise.
For him, and thousands like him,
the pain of the daily walk to work
is the only reality that exists,
unseen by the eyes of those driving by.

The Shame

The pain and the shame
of unemployment,
often seen as laziness,
another night, hungry and cold.
When, oh when, will the tide turn?

The Underworld

Deep in the caverns below, dark and treacherous,
Many have succumbed, gasping for breath.
Trapped forever, they remain buried,
Hidden behind unforgiving rocks.
Lonely ghosts searching for exits,
Gold clutched in hand.

This precious treasure enriched the owners,
Never the mine worker.
A trading commodity to the world,
A hope for a future not drowning in poverty.
The mining towns now lay bare.

There's a second rush, it seems,
Illicit operations on the fringe of old mines.
New shanty towns rise.
The lure of gold and promised riches
Still pulls many deep into the belly of the earth.
Many new lost souls crossing paths with the old.

Moment of Peace

Land desolate and bare,
every day, a struggle
to survive, to live.
Yet upwards we gaze,
the rays of hope
beating against silent prayers
for a moment of peace,
one moment of solace.

The Migrant

Swimming towards a new life,
the promised land,
only the strongest survive.

Wild Thoughts

The dust and sand rising against the wind,
blurring vision, demanding focus.
Running riot, rudderless in a stormy sea,
a thousand thoughts galloping through my mind,
causing chaos in my heart and soul.

Untamed Fire

This is too late
In the danger zone already
Livid, spewing expletives
Baying for blood
My prayer is that I don't
Meet the offender
My anger will be fuel
For an untamed fire

Anger

The anger rages like a river,
In torrential flood, relentless.
A pit full of serpents, the red flags ignored.
Spirit saying be kinder, help, show love,
Forgive even the unforgivable.

All of which is thrown back with such vengeance,
Spitting flames and dripping blood.
As you hack away at my soul, like Ravana itself.

I walk away now, grieving and heartbroken,
For I lost myself in the madness of trying
To be the better person, in a room filled with
Lecherous poison called family.

Ageing Parents

The moments I can't breathe,
So many in a day,
So much happening,
So little understanding.

It's easy to watch from the sidelines
And not be in the game,
To give commentary and opinions
With no inputs or solutions.

It's something I never understood
And still don't, don't think I ever will.

Where is the rulebook that says
The responsibility is mine to bear alone,
To be the sole caregiver of our aged parent?
Is she not your parent too?

My Dad's Story

A labourer, which is what he was, back in the day,
raised a family of five, plus the wife.
Never shirked on responsibility,
worked six days a week,
and then helped those around him.

There were those times, though,
that his cheery self faded,
and he became despondent and sad.
They said he was mad; sent him to hospital.
They kept him chained to his bed,
tried new medication and altered dosages.
It was too pitiful to see.

Then he would come home, back to work,
the family person, and everything was alright.
This went on for most of his life.
Some only know of him because of his illness,
undiagnosed correctly right to the end.
I knew him well enough to know him,
not as mad, but as my dad.

The Pain of a Father

One saw the pain in those eyes
long before the broken body.
Random thoughts in earlier years,
Surely, even a donkey doesn't toil so hard.

The promises of rest in his golden years,
those dreams ripped into shreds by the selfish son.
The father never said no,
not because he could not,
he dared not risk losing his only child.
So, he worked harder and longer,
always just a bit more.

That same son, in a heartbeat, didn't think twice
to shove the old man aside.
"I've got my own life to live,
I cannot be burdened with your aches and pains."

The story of the father, who once stood tall,
sheltering the son from the storms,
withered and wilted from the lack of love or care.
And when the body finally succumbed
to that last wheezing breath,
it was not hard to see that
the soul had been crushed a long time ago.

The Sick Body

A body riddled with disease is no home for the soul.
Watching someone we love wither away is painful.
We pray for healing and recovery.
We beg and plead with doctors,
Make deals with God,
Fervently clutching at straws for any miracle.
When that moment comes, yes, there is absolute sadness.
Our tears are unabated.
The loss seems too much to bear.
Within all of this, there is a sense of relief,
Although we do not speak of it.
Relief because the suffering has ended,
Suffering for the one that has been ill for so long,
Suffering that we endured watching our loved one,
And knowing in our soul that there was no miracle waiting.

Sorry is a Sad Word

In that moment of time,
the pain was excruciating.
My mind questioning,
my soul looking for answers.

I faded from your thoughts.
Days rolled into weeks,
weeks into months.

You felt relieved that it was
not you in this deep pain.
Unable to understand my loss,
the best you could do was "Sorry."

Broken Children

Children carry the weight of the world,
imposed by broken adults,
struggling with holding up the façade
or breaking down the walls.

Family

We grow up within the confines
Of how we were raised,
The family values, the stories told,
Of what exists within the walls of the home.
What we see, what we hear, what we say,
That creates an impression on us.
What we are sheltered from,
What we are allowed to feel,
What secrets the family harbours and hides.
We fear the same things our parents did,
We love the same things our parents do.
Sometimes we break out of this mould,
We rebel and move out of this norm.
We fall, we rise, but we find
That something, that feels truer to us.
That is when this becoming true to ourselves
Is seen as defiance by parents and society.
We become the black sheep, we are ousted.
We find ourselves alone, no family to call our own.
We find ourselves a new tribe,
Of like-minded souls,
Those that were not afraid
To break free from what we were told.

May children be loved but not moulded,
May children be safe but not chained,
May children be guided but not stifled.

Mothering

It is in the softest of sighs, watching with bated breath,
As the eyes reach the gates in the excitement of the reunion,
The apprehension of the chaos that ensues.
It's knowing that there is love tinged with rough words,
Casually thrown in a moment of despair.

Mothering is not for the faint-hearted.
It is worse for the child,
Where the essence of nurturing has been
Lost in the social ills of our streets.

Alone is Not Lonely

My soul seeks the solitude,
for it is only in the silence
that I can listen to myself.
The silence is deafening.

For in those moments,
the truth hurtles forward,
demanding I stay still,
facing my fears, feeling the pain.
Waves of emotion thrown out,
without prying eyes or judgement.

The soul knows long before the heart listens,
and the mind accepts as peace settles in, as night falls,
and hope grows as a new day rises.

The Apology

These recent weeks, months, years even,
Have crushed my soul.
The apologies that are necessary
I know will never come.
I must pick me up,
Dust the cobwebs of my plans,
Heal and fix my broken pieces,
And step gently back into life.

The End

I tried everything
Be patient, they said
Speak kindly, be gentle
He will come around

But still you faded away
Always out of reach
And finally gone forever

The Bridge

The bridge that once existed,
dangling in the wind,
standing at the edge of a cliff,
no one to hold me back,
no one to say, "please don't."
Out of desperation,
no hope in sight,
leaving unanswered questions
and an incomplete story.

Dark Thoughts

In the deep of the night,
thoughts run rampant.
The silence is shattered.
When dawn comes,
like crickets, they retreat,
and all seems well again.

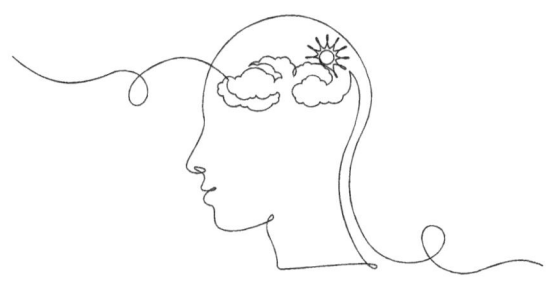

Your Eyes Deceived Me

Looking through your lenses,
All I see is me, your version of me,
A defeated me, a deflated me,
Staring back with empty eyes.

Back then, I was drowning,
swallowed by quicksand.
The more I struggled,
the more I disappeared.

One day, I stopped.
I stopped fighting,
I stopped caring.

I was hoping for a definitive end.

And slowly, the grip released.
I finally see me through my own eyes.

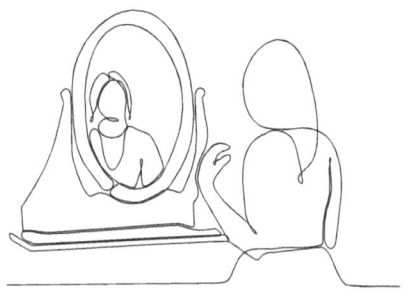

Safe Space

My heart was mine, still is, I am told.
I stepped into your world,
young, crazy "in love,"
and my soul feeling like I have known you before.

Unaware that loving you did not mean
that I had to give my whole self away,
I made you my world, my sun, and my moon.
My entire being breathed so that you could be at peace.

I stand back now, pained over the years,
watching the battering my soul has taken, it still does.
I seek healing every day, through tears,
laughter here and there.

I see now that you had a houseful of baggage,
and I walked in with my bags too.
I thought we could fix each other.

Not realising that whilst I would eventually face my monsters,
you were not able to, I could not fix your missing pieces
without you wanting them fixed.

Darkness

Darkness hovers not too far.
The moon, it is there some nights.
Other nights, only the stars give comfort.
Sometimes the night is too long.
The sun will come up.
When, is the question.
If I am brave, I see the light sooner,
but when the fear persists,
so too does the darkness.

The Waves

Waves playfully racing to kiss the shoreline,
washing away the footprints of lovers walking by.
White, fluffy foam lingering a bit,
driftwood tossed around teasingly.
The sun and the moon basking on the ocean's face.

Sometimes there's a sensing,
other times without warning.

Grey and moody, the saltiness stings.
The waves come thundering, crashing on the shore,
ripping into the beach, grabbing everything within reach,
clawing it back into the ocean.

The next waves come, relentless,
spitting out the remnants of what doesn't get sucked
into the deep realms of the ocean.
The ebb and flow of the ocean,
the smooth sailing and stormy seas of life.

The Book

And life changes forever.
From the preface, the new owner realised,
That this was no ordinary book.
Page after page, it became more difficult
To separate the story from her life.
Random strangers arriving in her home.
Did she let them in,
Or were they always here?
Why was the hall closet door always open?
She's sure she has seen a light in there, even heard voices.

The Bench

The bench is well placed,
Just to gaze across the dancing grass.
The sun and wind kissing me gently,
Feeling loved, I can walk back.
Other days, I want to walk on,
Ignoring the bench that beckons me,
Pretending I do not feel the sun or the wind.
Over and yonder, I know I will not look back.

Run Through the Rain

I want to run through the rain,
To feel it soak through my skin,
So that the tears streaming down my face
Seem nothing more than raindrops.
The gut-wrenching screams stuck in my throat
Seem nothing more than gleeful shrieks
Of running in the rain.

I want to run in the rain,
For I cannot cry without tears,
Nor can I keep my screams on silent.
I want to run in the rain, to end the pain.

Like the Lotus

My life is murky,
a lot of hurting and healing.
I try to stand tall,
hesitant, one foot in, one foot out.
No safe space to rise
like the lotus from the mud.
Reminders of the me from before,
not enough of who I truly am.

Flame the Sparks

The sparks ignited,
Flames burning so bright.
Surely this was forever.
We never saw it coming,
Drifting in a leaky boat.
Life seemed to happen,
The fire fizzled out.
We are left with only
What could have been.

Roadblocks

The Universe has spoken.
Planetary influences are too great to ignore.
The stars are not aligned; it is an impossible match.
Roadblocks and hurdles, no prospective future,
Can be read in the horoscopes for the forlorn couple.
Can love win when destiny is written in the skies?

The Dark

Darkness swallows up even the light
Of the stars or moon.
Shadows of trees standing tall,
Unwavering, afraid to move.
A flutter and a swoosh,
Maybe just an owl,
The softest rustle of the ground.

I reached up slowly,
Standing tall, unfurling my light
Like a flag in the wind.

Soon the trees too will sway,
And birds will wake,
Light will be around.

Hidden Abuse

She was told not to let them know
what happens inside the family home.
Lies told to her friends and the neighbours,
everyone saw the smiling faces,
the cheerful façade of the family.
Nobody saying aloud
what they suspected for a while.
Chilling horror, the day they found her,
bruised and broken, ended the pain,
a rope twisted out of that fancy
wedding saree she wore barely a year ago.

Failing Our Women and Children

Every day I pray as I repost a missing person report,
in the hope that the family is reunited with their loved one.

Every day without fail, reposts from days before
surface in timelines as "found deceased."

It's always women; old and young, and children
who just fade away into the darkness without any signs.

Why, oh, why is it always our sisters and children
that are brutally robbed of life?

Children with dreams; young women succeeding at studies,
ready to launch into their chosen careers.

Mothers waiting to celebrate their young one's achievements,
grannies telling the whole village of the first doctor in
generations.

It is always the jealous lover or the estranged husband.
It is always a man who crushes hopes, dreams, and souls.

Women's Day

Humans reaching for the stars,
delving into the vast oceans,
in the name of progress.
Women, pivotal to the success,
made in a man's world.

Yet women are still chained
by outdated ideas and opinions.
"Keep them reined in," they say.
Seems we need to be tamed,
for left unchecked,
we are wild and difficult.
Little girl children to grandmothers,
all subjected to a patriarchal world.

We tell our daughters to fly,
but only as high as a man allows,
so as not to make him feel any less of a man.
The woman who tries to free herself
from the shackles of social conditioning is brave,
for then she is often beaten or killed
for wanting to be more.

May the day come when we can just be all that society needs,
without losing the essence of being ourselves,
where we are not forced to fit into moulds
created by a society that does not fully understand
that an empowered woman is not the enemy,
but the strongest ally needed
To turn this ship to calmer waters.

End the World

The world should just implode; reset from ground zero.
Too much turmoil and no peace in sight,
egos getting in the way of humanity,
people at war with themselves.

Or we could all just STOP for one moment in time
and choose peace over war.

Diwali

The world is hurtling into chaos,
Irreversible perhaps,
Pain ripping souls open,
The atrocities too ghastly.
Trying to find a reason to
Celebrate my small wins
Seems so selfish,
When the woes of the world
Are so devastating.

Diwali comes around on a dark night
To remind me that faith and hope cannot be fickle,
To trust the power of light over dark,
And good over evil.

Fireworks

The stadium erupts in a kaleidoscope of light,
to celebrate the sports win.
Every hue, every shade,
the pyrotechnics are spectacular.
No environmentalists up in arms,
raising awareness on pollution.

New Year's Eve, parties galore,
it's like the Carnival in Rio.
Rockets and flares, showers of light,
noisy bangers too,
welcomes the new year in.
No complaints though, no sleeping babies disturbed,
or dogs that go berserk.
It's the spirit of the celebrations.

Guy Fawkes Night,
people wilding everywhere.
Why did we take on this very British day
to all corners of the world?
Sadly, incidents occur of maiming pets in drunken stupor.

The festival of lights – Diwali – the Indian Christmas.
Rows of lamps, light over darkness,
the fireworks displays, small or big.
The noise dispels the evil,
and the light chases away the dark.
Yes, it's exam time, and it disturbs the studious.
It pollutes the air and streets.
Once day breaks, kids will scurry around looking for
unburnt fireworks, and clean up too.
And the dogs will still hate it.
There's always an uproar
about fireworks over Diwali.
It is so loud only at this time, I wonder why?

Christmas

Tree reaching out to the high roof,
adorned with dazzling lights and traditional trinkets,
artfully wrapped gifts adorning its base,
elaborate menus planned with festive cheer,
Christmas songs playing everywhere,
Santa Claus is coming to town.

Last-minute dash to the stores,
tripping over the street waifs,
muttering in annoyance,
barely noticing kids with the sad eyes,
shivering in the cold,
drenched in the smell of the streets.

Packages in hand, eyes turned away,
we walk pretending not to see
the failing of society and
the failing of humanity.

Christmas Madness

Mesmerising and hypnotic, it draws the beholder in,
The twinkle of the lights, garish and abhorrent,
Frenzied madness on the streets.

Tinsel, baubles, gifts and food; the obscenity of it all,
Elaborate wrapping flying in the wind.
New toys soon discarded as boredom sets in.
Tables bearing down on the weight of the food,
Gluttony rolls around unashamedly.

No thought of the ones on the fringes of society,
Who look towards the lights flickering in the distant near,
Not so much as a caring look towards the beggar on the street.
It's always disdain, disgust and utter repulsion,
Sometimes a casually thrown dollar bill or a food parcel,
Just for ticking off the charity box.

Families circle back to each other,
Seated at elaborate tables, cheerfully decorated.
Food and drink aplenty – too much for a table this size.
Holiday banter and fake conversations,
Christmas photos and selfies all over – others wishing for the same.
Some harshness creeps through,
And slowly everyone retracts to their own little lives,
Grateful that this annual façade is over till the next year.

The Flour Massacre

Thousands waited on prayers and hope
for the next food drop,
flour and almost nothing else,
turned into meals for the starving.

The oppressors eagerly told the world
it was a stampede by the mob,
an unruly bunch, determined to loot aid trucks.
When the mushroom cloud finally dissipated over Hiroshima,
the gruesome truth of the atomic bomb unfolded.
Likewise, in Al-Rashid, when the dust settled,
it was gunfire that killed hundreds,
not a wild scramble for food.
Shoot and kill, maim and destroy,
taunt and hunt,
an ego-filled madness has consumed the oppressors.

Train Tracks

Tracks that once stood firm,
Connecting friends and family,
People and places,
Taking the farm to the city,
And bringing the cities to the farm.
Broken and rundown,
Desolate and bare,
From the lack of care.
The human network too
Breaks down from neglect,
Beyond repair.
All that remains are the
Memories of what once was.

Don't Talk to Me

Don't talk to me about trauma,
or anxiety levels that are so high
that you have no courage.
Don't tell me about your day,
where you feel so under pressure,
like giving up seems the answer.
Don't ask me for the world,
just because you can.

Talk to me about missiles falling
on homes, hospitals, and schools,
about families lying under rubble,
days after the buildings crumbled.
Dead or alive, nobody knows.

Talk to me about children
who will be traumatised for life,
who are the last of their family line,
who are alive, but limbless.

Talk to me about the mothers
begging soldiers to leave their children alone,
who watch while their families
are butchered in front of them.
Talk to me about the rapes, the killings,
the brutality, about the forgotten children of Gaza.

Eyes that Plead... Part 1

Eyes searching the dusty haze, heart pounding.
Every breath washed by a sea of anxiousness.
Their world crumbles as they watch,
buildings caving under the weight of the missile strikes,
ferocious and deadly,
snuffing the lives of so many others just like them.
Like flames in the wind, a gush brings intensity
and leaves smouldering rubble,
charred bodies remain, faceless and forlorn.

The young man, racing to the sanctity of their love,
a conscious risk, a movie in his mind,
seeing only her eyes that plead for the nightmare to end.
Over the deafening thunder
of the raucous laughs of the enemy,
he heard the wind carrying the bullets marked for him.
Cowardly, the empty shell of the soldier hit him from behind.
He felt the burn ripping into his back
and exploding in his heart.
His fears, hopes, and dreams died
in one fell swoop, crushed into oblivion.

Eyes that Plead... Part 2

He could not call out the name of his Divine,
nor scream for the love of his life.
Open sluices in flood, the blood gushing—
unabated, swirling in a dusty path.

A Hindu would have said Vetri Vel Muruga,
the white peacock, beautifully strange,
unfamiliar in the killing fields of Gaza.
Almost blissful and serene,
in the chaos of a world gone mad.
Wings gently enveloping our martyred son,
like a mother cradles her newborn.

The body ceases to twitch, the crimson tide now a trickle.
Eyes reach to the heavens,
rescuers turning upward to say a dua for the blessed soul,
leaving in the divine chariot.

Tsunami

What is this madness?
This tsunami of warfare,
Like molten lava, spewing across
The tiny land, crushing everything without remorse.
The warlords supporting the massacres,
Defying the rules of the civilised nations.
Across the world, there is a revolution rising,
First world citizens becoming
Enemies of their own states,
The oppressors' own kindred
Standing up against power-hungry leaders.
Ceasefire,
Ceasefire,
Ceasefire.

Will the madness end in this lifetime?
Or will it be the end of us all?

God's Forgotten Children

A tiny piece of land
that nations scramble over.
There is nothing there,
no oil and gas, or fields of crop to sell.
No homes intact, no school or hospital,
all blown up by terror attacks.

From above Earth,
there are no fences to be seen,
yet the Palestinian cannot live in peace
in this place he calls home.
Nor can he move, with family in tow,
to any neighbouring land.
Though they call themselves Muslim,
their borders remain closed.
The western world shuns them,
terrorists they say, in ignorance,
confusing the radicals and the ordinary man.
Now they stand with the oppressor,
sending weaponry to destroy a perceived threat.

There's bloodshed and pain,
the stench of death is ever lingering,
the wails of mourning pierce the soul.

Tears flow from the land to the sea,
as does the blood
of people who just want a place
they can call home.

God too, it seems, has forgotten the people
in the killing fields of Gaza.

The Story of Two Sides

How many days have passed?
206 days, depending on where one counts from,

Was the world always silent?
A feeble whimper here and there?
Or were the protests always ignored?

We are fighting for our right to life.
We are fighting against the oppression of our people.

You are holding our people hostage.
You have been killing our people with brute force.

We will not back down.
We will not surrender.

Both sides of the same coin,
Leaving thousands dead,
Maimed for life and generations wiped out.
Each side adamant to continue the fight.

Who will put down the weapons first?
How many days before there is surrender,
Or peace, or total annihilation?

The Promised Land

Walking through the ravaged land,
there are those who continue to search
amongst the rubble for the promised future.

Trotting over broken glass,
not feeling the pain or seeing the blood,
while searching for life
and grieving the dead.
They'll see the new homes
that will be built in the days to come.

Death, they know all too well.
Its impending appearance comes
through missiles and airstrikes
and brute ground force.
Families killed and others maimed,
the survivors live for another moment,
waiting for the terror and destruction to end,
to start anew again.

New Moon

The night is still dark, but the Moon starts to show its face.
Tiny slivers of light cut through the clouds.
A sense of hope – face to face with the pain.
We find solace in the comfort of the growing moon.

Speck of Light

It may be dark, though I am never alone.
Tiny specks of light all around me.
When I open my soul, I too am a speck of light,
For another being that feels the dark.

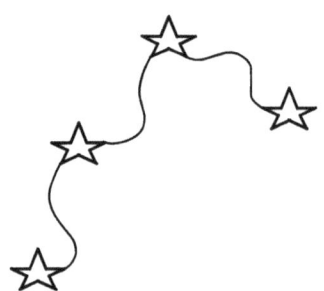

Rise

Somewhere stuck in the crevices of my soul,
I always knew I could never remain in pain.
A gnawing at my core,
To rise above this abandonment,
To accept that my path
In this lifetime is greater.

Layers

In the perfect world,
Perfection itself is admired.
Peel away the layers,
A different clarity appears.
It is impossible to keep hidden,
And can never be forgotten.

The Painting

The painting remains unfinished,
Each stroke, the softest caress,
Or heavy-handed in brutality.
A new dimension of depth,
And a layer removed.
Appraised in the future
As a masterpiece or a failure,
The painting remains unfinished
Till you breathe your last.

The Canvas

The brush flies across the canvas,
In swift streaks and dainty lines.
Bold and bright or subdued and dull,
A story with each kiss of brush to palette.

In the hands of the wicked, a cursed fable will be told.
In the hands of the honorable,
Your greatness will be emboldened.
Choose with care the person
Who gets to paint your life story.

Waves of Pain

We float between the pain and healing,
reflecting on how far we have traversed,
even though there are still waves of pain.

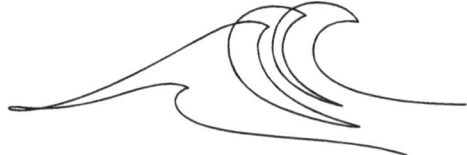

The Dance

The pain comes in waves,
Just gnawing at the surface,
Enough to trigger
A fight or flight response.

In the eye of the storm,
Clawing back with every
Reserve ounce of strength.

In the dance of healing,
It is step forward, step forward,
Step back,
Step forward, step back.

Strangers

Back there in the mist,
He stood still,
Lost in thought,
Lost in the haze.
The one who barely looked up,
But had greeted in subdued tones.

Who is he, I wondered?
Where are his loved ones?
Does he have a home?

Strangers we are,
As we pass each other in life,
Sometimes kind, sometimes cruel.
So many untold stories,
And many unknown mysteries,
Yet paths that cross in strange ways.

Grateful for You

Strangers in the wind,
Just names, a picture or two.
So many stories, some told,
Some yet to be told.
Each has brought something to the table,
Some: witty, thought-provoking words,
Others: words to boost my spirit,
A cheerful good morning,
And beautiful prayers to soothe the soul.
We laugh over the calamity of our country,
We cry over its destruction together.
It is the kind of relationship that
Has just enough to help us make
It through each day.

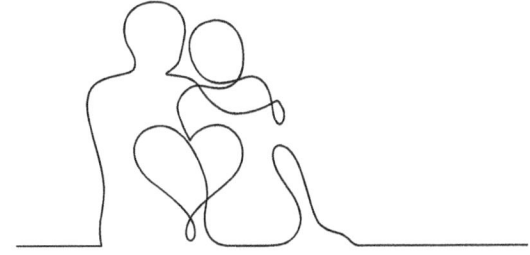

Light Back to You

Do not fear,
Look around you,
Trust your soul.
Even when you fall,
There will still be light
To catch you,
To help you rise,
To help you soar.
For trusting your soul,
You give strength to yourself.
For trusting your soul,
You bring light back to you.

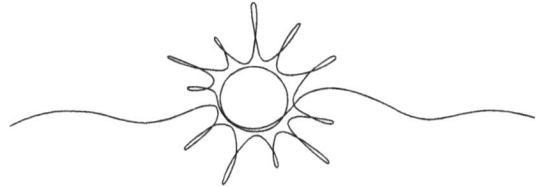

The Sun

At times I just want to breathe,
To gaze into the first light,
Hues of pink creeping through the dark,
Or watch the sun turn into a ball of fire,
As it sinks into the horizon.

Free

Feet kissing the ground,
Wind in my hair,
No fear of reprisal.
A gentle canter,
Or a heart-pounding ride.
I yearn for the days
When I can be free.

The Soul

As the breath fades away,
The soul stands naked,
Sheer light, too bright,
Or frail and fragile.
At that time, as the body falls away,
The soul may fight to stay,
Yet it knows it must go.

As I Die

I want to reach out to hold you tight, like we used to.
Those hugs that made everything alright.
My soul is torn between staying
Or moving on towards the light.
My soul knows enough; I've done this before
In another lifetime – I cannot stay,
For a homeless soul will wander about aimlessly.

Twirl of Words

My voice is soft and soothing,
My words lure you in,
My beauty mesmerises you,
Dainty, fragile, gentle,
You cannot look away.

The colours of the cloth,
They dance by themselves,
Swaying and swirling,
Keeping you entranced.

Do not let your guard down, though,
For the pain you caused me,
And the fire that rages deep in my soul,
Will fell you, with one fearsome twirl of words.
Beauty and colour.

Strong One

Just because I seem to have it together,
That I seem to have handled my losses well,
That I seem to have gotten on with life,
That I seem strong and resilient,
That I seem to bounce back easily,
Does not mean that I am truly okay.

I've had to get back on the horse,
Cry in secret,
Pretend I'm over the grief,
Get on with life,
Be strong and resilient,
Bounce back with each knock,
Because I had to be there for you.

Just know that every strong person
Needs a moment too in life,
Where they can be frail,
Need love and care,
Be broken for that time,
Where a hug may be all that's truly needed.

I hope in that moment of time,
That you can be there for your strong one.

Desolate

Stark and desolate,
Bare and barren,
So, it seems,
Just unending plains
Meeting hills and mountains.
The barrier and tar show,
Though that man has passed here.

Misunderstanding

Alone and lost, misunderstood,
Silent conversations in my head.
Lost in my thoughts of aloneness and self-pity,
I drift along the stormy seas in the busyness of life.
I feel unloved, not realising I mirror your soul too.

I force my soul to sit with my emotions,
Tossing each one around, intimately.
Looking at my lover, my friend,
And seeing the same pain there.

Slowly, I put my guard down
And seek out the gentle love that always existed.
We fall into each other,
The tenderness of the embrace is all too familiar.
The feeling of home as our lips meet
And our bodies melt into one.
We fell apart, but our souls remain entwined.

Dilemma

My cat sits still, sensing the air of discord.
With a swoosh of my wand and a bubbling cauldron,
All this could go away.
But then I close my eyes and remember,
If I delve in the dark, I could never be
In the light again.

Prison

Stars see the truth,
Even when the sky is empty.
From the deepest realms of your dark soul,
Truth will stretch out to free
Itself from the prison of your heart.

Today

May today be a day when I realise
That I stayed too long
In this mess called family,
Where all I did was accept
For not having somewhere else to go.

Today, though, I realise that I rose through it all.
I can walk away, not in pain,
But with grace and ease.

The Sacrifice of Self

So cliché,
Soft, sweet, understanding.

Below the surface,
A pot of bubbling emotions,
The sacrifice of self.

Motherhood brings untold joy,
It brings sadness, pain, and fear too.

When children go astray,
How to bring them home?

A child gone wild
Will blame the mother,
Not enough love, no support.

Battles and blame,
Till one day, you have your own bundle of joy,
And through those living years,
You see that mothering
Is not for the weak or faint-hearted.

Mother's Heart

A mother's heart never sleeps.
Her heartbeat wanders to her children.
The wind carries her love to them in their dreams,
And brings back their fears, sadness, and sorrow,
So that tomorrow, they can rise
with lighter hearts and new hope.

In the Eyes of the Father

Some people look for errors and mistakes,
While others look for beauty and inspiration.
And we usually find what we're looking for,
Only in the eyes of a father.
My hopes, my dreams, my fears.
It was not my mistakes and fears I saw there,
But he wanting to steer me away
From the pain of the lessons that followed.
I look at my children's father,
And I see in his eyes the same and more.
A good father always wants more for his children.
In his eyes, you will see his hopes and dreams.

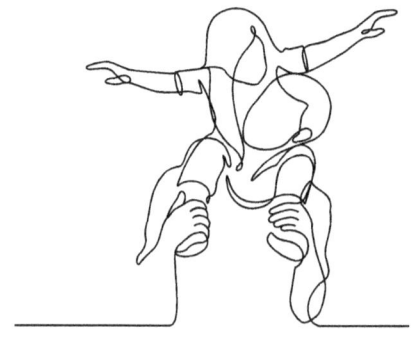

Shards of Me

A prisoner of thoughts and beliefs,
Which did not always make sense.
Plodding through life in chains and harness,
Unable to breathe, live, laugh,
Without approval.

Without your approval, that is.
You groomed me like a pet project,
To control, handle, and mishandle.
Conditioned me to believe that this is how it should be.

Not expecting, not believing,
That my life could be anything more
Than you made it out to be.

One day the glass box broke,
I could not even recall how, but it did.
Fragmented shards of all I ever knew about myself,
Strewn about, like a jigsaw puzzle with missing pieces.

A myriad of strangers
Lovingly glued the broken bits,
With tenderness I didn't understand,
Into a mosaic that stands strong today.

I learned that I didn't have to fit into any box,
Not yours or mine or anyone else's ever again.
I can keep building and breaking,
Breaking and building, without judging myself.

For the lost years, the work is in progress,
And the masterpiece that is yet to come.
I breathe, laugh, and cry these days,
A tinge hesitantly, but without looking up for approval.

Run Free

The one with the harness
Broke free from its shackles.
A life of luxury, good food,
Personal groomsmen,
Vet on standby.

It needed to run free
And feel the wind in its mane,
Without having a whip
Beat down its side,
To win another race.

We all need to be
The one who breaks free.

Breaking Free

Dark, ugly words, painfully cruel,
Barricade behind lock and key,
Caged in for decades,
Impossible to be free.
The mirror screams back.

At the edge of the precipice,
Dangerously close to falling,
A hand reached out, a little hand.

You look kind, can you help me?
My brain is saying no, I am not a nice person.
The little voice says again, yes, you can help me.
How, my brain asks?

My heart feels it knows
How to finally break free.

Unharnessed Thoughts

Horses gallop in wild abandon,
Unharnessed and free.
No riders to rein them in
To a gentle canter.

Thoughts thundering by,
Without restraint,
Bringing on another night
Where sleep evades me.

Wild Horses

A thousand wild horses in a desert sandstorm,
The old crashing into an unfathomable mess.
Change hurls one into a hurricane of chaos,
A piece of driftwood in an untamed sea.

The old falls away as the dust settles,
And the wind dies down.
One unfurls like a new leaf.
There's a faint tinge of familiarity,
Humble acceptance of the new.

The Smoke that Thunders

Some gleeful shrieks,
Rainbows spray around.
Foliage reaches out, wisps of damp.
The mist shrouds the view.

The thunderous roar, then lo and behold,
The mighty Zambezi as it crashes below.
Victoria Falls, mighty and ferocious.
The walk through the rainforest
To the Smoke that Thunders.

The Sea

Looking across,
The waves gently
Lapping my feet.
There's a nagging urge.

I could sail, I feel,
Into the sunset
Or a new sunrise.

The sea can be ferocious,
Life can be brutal.
I use the soft waves
To get a little ahead.

Stormy Seas

I don't wear my scars with shame.
Skull and bones bring you no fame.
I've stayed afloat in treacherous seas,
With strange creatures wishing to pull me under.

Many a time, I've been on top,
Trusting the hand that reached out to help,
Instead, being pushed under again.
Like a buoy, I keep surfacing.

Soon these storms will fade,
And then I'll frolic like the dolphin
In a calm bay.

Sandy Shores

Looking back on all the times I could not swim,
Could not take myself back to shore,
I didn't stop myself from plunging into the deep darkness.

And then I think of those brave ones
Who dived right in, dragging me back up for air,
And who kept me afloat through the storms,
Till my feet touched the soft sandy shores.

Winds of Change

Throw me to the wolves,
Or make me the villain.
Detract from the problem,
Ignore the true monster.
I have been hurled
Into the winds of change
Many times before.
Each time, I rise,
More refined than before.
This time will be no different.
I have no fear or regrets
Of walking the next steps on my own.

I Rise Again

Shadows reach out,
Creeping and stretching.
Darkness tries, in many ways.

My soul stirs and roars,
And from the ash, I rise again,
Breathing fire,
And burning all that
Is not meant to be.

The Phoenix Rising

The Phoenix rises from the ash,
Resilient, never backing down,
Overcoming challenges,
Always with a positive outlook.

Far from easy to always be strong,
To always look forward,
Realism is knowing that the strong
Breaks you down too.
Prayer warriors don't always bring the answers,
Empaths too need support and care.

The Phoenix does not rise from the ash.
Sometimes the Phoenix is the fire.

Hope

Brittle and bare, skeletal in nature,
Waiting for some respite,
Craving revival, hoping for care.
The mystery of nature,
A wisp of a blossom, then more.
No rain to wash off the dust.
Slow signs of life,
A gush deep in my soul,
No longer withering,
Alive with hope.

Grow

Do not let the situation define you.
This environment is a temporary restraint.
Grow out of the cracks;
defy and refuse to conform.
Grow and escape
the mundane madness that surrounds you.

The Forest Lives

In the underworld down below,
It is clammy and cold,
Yet the forest is alive,
From light that streams in.

Nature

We are spoilt, and I am always amazed
That even without rain,
the new leaves and buds come anew.
Nature functions without man's intervention.

Rain

The smell of the earth,
The moisture, cool on my skin,
The first few raindrops,
A promise of renewed growth
Or the fear of the destruction that follows.

The Same Ones

It is always the same,
The same ones who do,
Who build and rebuild,
Who reach out and mend.

The same ones who don't,
Who break and destroy,
Who stand back and watch.

Some learn along the way,
Others fall through the hole.

Race Against Time

It's a race against time, in this lifetime,
To undo the past and build for the next.
Souls spinning the karmic wheel,
Trying to undo eons of karmic debt
In this single breath.

We take on mammoth tasks at every turn,
Competing with each other,
Serving humanity and saving the world.
We overextend ourselves, becoming martyrs.
Every waking moment cannot be for the good of others only.
Serve yourself well first and do a little good every day,
With what you have in this moment of time,
For just one other soul.
This is how you redeem yourself against the circle of life.

Transitions

When a good person transits,
That is the hardest to accept.
That is the end of all
The goodness that existed between us.
The memories will always remain,
And the link is forever etched into eternity.

Memories

There is a faint tug in my soul,
Enough to make me sombre,
Not enough to make me weep.
Does that mean I love you less?
I know your journey here with me has ended,
And no soul, no matter the love,
Can hold one back for selfish gain.
A thousand memories and enough synchronicities
To know that I was loved,
To know that I am loved.

The Dance of Words

"Our eyes meet,
over the dancing heads of the lavender and English roses.
Captivated, our souls fall in love.
We waltz through seasonal balls,
The moon and the stars seducing us into dreamy intimacy.

The winds bring the whispers.
In hushed tones, we speak of the war that is coming.
My beau joins the others at the border,
armed and ready for combat.
I am a medical nurse, the horrors of those brought back,
etched in my mind.
Every day that my beau is not amongst those
with missing limbs that arrive at the infirmary, I am grateful.
I am petrified too.

Days turn into weeks and weeks into months.
News drizzles in and out,
Missing soldiers, many fallen heroes,
Mostly prisoners of war..."

There is a sequel.
With greedy hands, heart, and soul,
I picked up from where I left off.
Do lovers reunite?
I cannot wait to find out.

Space

Space, dark and silent,
Rock debris floating by, crashing here and there.
The planets moving in unison,
Knowing their path,
Separately but together.
The sun and moons dance,
In rhythm, in this vastness
We call space.
Stars flicker, some bright, some fade too soon,
Looming out and beyond.
There is Earth, peeping through the clouds.
In this greatness, Earth looks upwards,
A small wonder in this universe.
This universe is only one of many yet unknown.
To think that we are mere specks of stardust,
Gravitating to life, on this here, our Earth.

The Universal Thread

Is it egoistical, I ask,
To feel that one carries the Universe in your soul?
Or that there's a ribbon of cosmic energy
That connects our soul to the universe?

Some days it feels that I am weighted down
in unexplained pain.
On other days, I slay dragons with a magical sword.

What is this thread that ties me to you,
and to all the universes?

Rest

Dragging one's soul to the finish line,
Albeit a temporary respite.
Emotional turmoil,
The wretched chaos unhindered,
Sheer willpower or zombie mode.
There's a gentle whiff,
Sweet and inviting,
A promise of calm.
The silly season beckons,
Summer holidays on the horizon.

Warmer Days

Beautiful hues,
Gentle sway to the ground,
The rustle underfoot.

Soon the ice-blue skies
Will bring cold days
And icy nights.

Those that are of the street
Will feel the cold gnawing away,
As they try to keep warm
Under the plastic and cardboard.

Yet it will be me and you,
Who, though snug and warm,
Won't cease to long for warmer days again.

Just Go

I woke up before the birds today,
December, day two already.
I tell myself that I need to pick myself
Out of these doldrums.
This is not me, I bounce back.

I had plans to finish the year on a high,
I came to terms with losses,
I won at work, at my studies too,
I met beautiful people,
I made a difference.

Why did you come along
And rip my world into shreds?
You are not chained to my life,
The door is open – just go.

So that I can find my way
To myself again.
I deserve to finish the year on a high,
I owe this to myself.

Open Door

Bolted shut, heavy and dark.
Chained, impossible to open.
Defeated and squirming in quicksand,
A sense of safety in the darkness,
The comfort we do not want to shed,
Familiar like an old friend.
Courage falters and fades.
Doubt creeps in, cold and forlorn.
The universe is shaking up your world.
The light streaming in,
Slivers of hope whistling in the breeze.
Free falling, no parachute in sight.
Amid chaos, the open door remains obscured.
The mind is afraid of what may be.
Deep breaths and clutching at reserves,
To step out of the known to the unknown,
On the winds of hope and faith.

Tinsel and Glitter

Tinsel and glitter, shiny baubles all around,
Tall trees with heirloom décor,
The streets adorned with festive décor.

Yet I am forlorn.
I can't quite catch the emotions eating at my soul.
It's an overwhelming sense
That this is not right,
That the world has gone crazy
In a tragic way, unable to reset.

The destruction within homes and society at large,
Countries bullying each other,
Greed and corruption are insatiable.
The depravity within communities.
It seems almost vulgar
To be enjoying the festivities of the holidays.
One cannot fix the problems alone.
Am I supposed to also turn a blind eye?

Every time we look away,
We condone and accept the wrongs of the world.
Yes, I should be grateful and celebrate my life,
But my soul cannot shake off the thought we need to be more,
For ourselves and for everyone.
Although it does not sit well with my soul,
Merry Christmas and happy holidays.

Resolution

New Year, New Me.
No, I will not succumb to this.
I will live in this moment.
Every window has a picture, good or bad.
I will choose how to view it.
An opportunity, a new approach.
It can be beautiful and soul-lifting.
It can be sad and soul-crushing.
Beautiful – I will be grateful.
Sad – what can I do to make this better?
I choose to be mindful in the moment.

The Pain of Joy

As the old year gallops towards the new year,
I take time for myself, as I always do.
It is almost nostalgic, somewhat deep,
As I look at my year coming to an end.
There is a sense of excitement as I do my vision board,
Sometimes in my head, most times on my wall,
for the next year.

I look back, just to see what I am leaving behind.
A fond farewell almost,
Like when you leave a bad relationship.
There is a sense of loss, but mostly relief.

I need to revisit the pain
That overshadowed what should have been joy.
I cannot sit with the emotions just yet,
As the wound is still too raw.
One day I will, just not today.

To Just Be

The queen of the jungle
Needs time in the sun
To just be.

Not to be brave or resilient,
Or strong and fearsome,
But to just be.

A Tinge of Jealousy

I don't yearn for what you have,
Don't wish that it could be mine.
Grateful for what is for me.

Today is different.
I am a bit sad, maybe even jealous,
To have missed the beautiful sights
Of the aurora australis over Cape Town.
The Northern Lights, a one-day "I will" dream.
For now, let me make peace
And let my heart find joy through the eyes that saw.

The 3-Legged Pot

Nothing special, they said,
That is just a pot.
Uma Ntuli upheka iphuthu ne khabishi
Ebhodweni lesizulu.
Do not insult the pot,
Do not insult our people.

Women stood over it,
In the sweltering heat,
Song in hand, cooking for the village.
Borrowed by Oom Piet
To make his oxtail potjie,
Over biltong and brandewyn.
Uncle Saleem, who makes biryani for weddings,
An explosion of spices
For all occasions.
Community feeding these days,
Rows of steaming pots,
Feeding a child, feeding a nation.

That pot holds the hopes and dreams of our people,
Of a future so bright,
That the darkness of the past
May soon only be found in textbooks.
The pain in our souls will pierce less,
Soothed by the beating drums of a new dawn.

The fire will burn what separates us,
The pot will hold everything that unites us.
That nothing special pot is Heritage.

Africa

Our vast land, another continent,
Beautiful and green,
Barren but with riches underfoot.

We drew invisible fences
To keep each separate,
Each formidable on its own,
Collectively a force beyond reckoning.

We speak differently,
We eat differently,
We dress differently,
We let our differences separate us,
Rather than unite us, against the world.

If only Africa stood as one,
Instead of selling pieces of ourselves
Through our wealth, gold, and diamonds,
Maize, tea, and coffee.
If only our leaders saw Africa as a blessing,
Instead of a cheap pawn for self-greed.

Africa could have ruled the world.

Full Moon

A full face, the brightness holds one in awe.
Every sadness seems to be erased,
With the moon beaming down on Earth.
A sense of hope, faith restored.
The moon may disappear, but it does shine again.

The Moon

The tiniest sliver or the whole man on the moon,
Even when the skies remain dark,
Amidst a million stars lighting up the sky,
There is a different level of peace
When one gets lost in its beauty.
The mind wanders off to those gone before us,
The stars throw kisses down below.
Imagining loved ones sitting on the curve of the moon,
Beaming smiles downward,
The moon will always call me home to you.

Earth Child

My soul only thrives if I am
Outdoors, barefoot, in nature, under the sky.
I am such an Earth child.
When I do not see the grass, plants, and flowers,
Sun, moon, stars, and skies,
I cannot breathe.

Life Force

Unfathomable light years away,
A tiny speck of energy,
Across multiple galaxies,
Into the outermost of space,
Is held by an unnamed force
In the greater cosmic play.

At a sublime level,
Within my innermost core,
The same life force exists.
Where protons and neutrons,
Quarks and gluons come together
To keep this body of mine in motion.
An energy not understood,
But without which, we would cease to be.

Energy and Essence

Paths crossing across lifetimes,
Hearts and souls entwined,
Onward journeys that started long before this lifetime.
Strangers connected by energy and essence,
Healing each other through words told and untold.

We Are Human

Be discerning with your magic,
As you sprinkle pixie dust along the way.
Tend to gardens that are deserving,
For hearts must receive your kindness
In all its glory, as you intended.
It is easy for the cruel to break you.
We are human, after all.

Alignment

Alignment of the mind, body, and soul.
It is no different to that of
The sun, moon, and stars.

The Soul Knows

The soul craves peace,
A space to just be,
Thoughts drifting by,
Uninterrupted,
Staying at leisure.
Provoking, demanding,
New insights unfold
In the stillness.
The heart listens,
The mind accepts,
The soul knows.
Science may heal
An ailing body,
Nature will heal
A weary soul.

The Lotus

Enamoured by the beauty of the lotus,
The crimson pink reflecting off the water,
Dragonflies flitting from flower to flower.
Distracted by the serenity,
One forgets the mud beneath
That sturdies the beauty above.

Wildflower

The lonesome wildflower,
Or the heirloom rosebush,
The sunflower on the concrete freeway,
Or the landscaped carpet of color.
My soul is buoyant in joy
At every blossom.
Flowers are not for the dead,
But for the living, for they rise the spirit
And elevate the soul.

The Sunflower

Fields of golden colour,
It was always a marker
As we neared home.
They were yours,
You would say.
A little girl back then,
All grown up now,
A single sunflower
Takes my heart straight to you.
Daughter of mine,
My very own sunflower.

The Rose

Beautifully poised, I stand tall.
Mesmerising, I draw you in.
Don't lose yourself though,
In my sweet fragrance.

Queen, I am.
Admire all you want,
Never yours to own.

Kiss the Earth

Grass blades, green and soft,
My feet kiss the grass.
Colourful blossoms dancing,
The scent teasing me.
Heart buoyant with the flowers
And their heady scent.
My thoughts lulled into silence.

Glimmers

Without shame, I find fairies
In the light prisms cast on the walls,
Glimmers catching something shiny.
I talk about magic and play with a wand,
Granting wishes in wild abandon.
Cheerful greetings to the flowers and the birds,
Crystals give me superpowers.
I trust without questioning,
All wildly unbelievable,
But very believable,
As seen through the eyes of children.

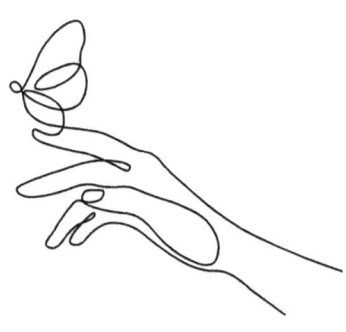

The Child in Me

As only a child can,
The flutter of a butterfly,
Images in the clouds,
Fairies and goblins.
A wildflower is precious,
A gift from secret friends.

A voice calls out to me,
Slowly, I turn around.
My face etched with years of wisdom,
My grey hair swinging gently.

"Grandma, I found one too."

The Rhythm of Life

The river doesn't struggle upward,
Over hills and mountains.
Instead, it meanders downwards,
Using the gradient of the land
To flow in torrential gushes
Or gentle streams.

Along the same natural paths
As it has done all the years before,
Or carving a new one, by gentle coaxing,
Not resisting, not demanding, no push or pull,
Till it reaches the ocean.

Learn to harness the power
Of not forcing the outcomes,
Working with the natural rhythm of things,
For therein lies the secret of true success.

Sunsets Are Made in Heaven

A palette in fiery orange,
Streaks of pink, or is that coral?
One of a kind, each masterpiece.
Blink and it is gone,
Its glory is for a chosen few,
Who await it with bated breath,
To catch a glimpse of this beauty
As day turns to night.

Pink Milkshake

There are days it is all that it is,
pink milkshake for you.
There will always be cuts
and bruises; scrapes and scars,
but those wounds are not you.
When those scars hurt and ache,
when you are told that they should not,

pour yourself pink milkshake,
pour love into yourself.

Home

Home is where I am,
Where my soul is free.
Not with the ones I love,
It is in the quietness of solitude.
When I am alone, I am not alone.
While the world sleeps,
Where my thoughts
Flow in wild abandon,
And my pains and joys are mine
To feel, without judging.
Home is where I can honour my soul
for all that I am.

Meditation

My quiet place,
Random thoughts,
A sensory explosion,
A flutter here, a buzz there.
I breathe in the stillness,
I breathe out the chaos.
Somewhere in between,
I pull myself to me.

Finding Oneself

Diving the depths of the ocean,
Launching into space,
Traveling the world,
Only to find oneself
Right here, right now.

Stillness

In that one moment in time,
It was perfectly peaceful.
The radiance of the night sky
Brought a stillness to my soul.

Silence

Let the world
Hear your silence,
And in that silence,
Hear your truth.

Holding Space

In the stillness of life, I breathe.
Deep and healing energy reaching into my core,
My soul is coming alive.
My mind is quiet now.
The cool water flowing over my feet,
The sun kisses me warmly,
The gentle flutter of the butterfly
Caressing me on the drift of the breeze.
To hold space for myself like this is top-tier self-care.
Somewhere in the distance,
The chime of the doorbell breaks my reverie,
And the spell is broken.

My Wings

It took me a long time
To realise that my arms
Could reach all the way around me.

I waited patiently for my turn,
For someone to help me.

But they are on now,
These wings of mine.

I fixed them on myself,
Straightened my crown,
And strode out into the world.

Unchained Soul

Try as you may,
All you chain are my hands.
My mind is free,
And my soul is mine.

Shakti

Fierce and bloodthirsty,
Pasted in yellow,
Vermillion thick tongue,
Eyes glazed and hair wild.

Mesmerized by love,
I fell under her spell.
My life in turmoil,
I reached out.
Oh Amma, my Divine Mother,
Help me, help me please.

Songs of devotion to her
Awakened my soul.
My body swayed,
Gentle at first,
Then with fervour.
I looked up to the sky,
Hands in prayer.
I said, "I accept Ma Shakti,
Lead me to oneness with you."

Later, I'm told,
When Amma moves me
In that trance state,
I am not fearful in composure,
But a gentle and compassionate
Extension of her love,
Sharing her messages
Of encouragement and comfort,
As only a mother can.

Mother of the universe,
Adi Shakti Parashakti.

Prayer

Grateful and blessed,
These hands of mine.
May the healing flow,
May the love flow,
In every which way,
Every single day.
To heal myself,
To help heal the world.

Hoarder, I Am

A hoarder I am, of things that may not make sense,
Squirreled away in my secret space.

Candles, charms, crystals and books galore,
Some reread to soothe my soul.
Different decades, telling a different story,
Others I have read a page, here and there,
Randomly picked out of the shelf,
Never dog-eared, a bookmark in place.

My favourite book? Is there even such a thing?

Crazy

Off you go now, little bee.
See you tomorrow,
glorious stars.
Crazy I may be,
talking to things
that can't answer back, it seems.
But they do, if you listen with your heart.

Jai Hind

Home, at last.
That is what it felt like.
My soul soared in excitement,
Tears flooded my face.

In that moment in time,
My senses told me I belonged.
Everything seemed so familiar,
Yet it was a first.

There was no sense of fear,
It was just an excitement that did not die down.
I truly felt that I had returned home,
To Mother's bosom, where my soul was loved.
Nothing has ever felt the same since.

As I stepped off that SAA flight
In Mumbai, a faded memory now.

Jai Hind, Mother India.

Road Trips

Childlike joy: no longer "when do we stop?"
Now, it is "what is next? What is that?"
My heart leaps and bounds
At the next bend, the next tree,
The next mountain or stream.
My soul can never be reined in.
I am only truly alive outside,
When the sun kisses my face,
Or the wind ruffles up my hair,
Or the moon shines down on me,
Or the stars flicker from above.
Open roads bring me back to me.

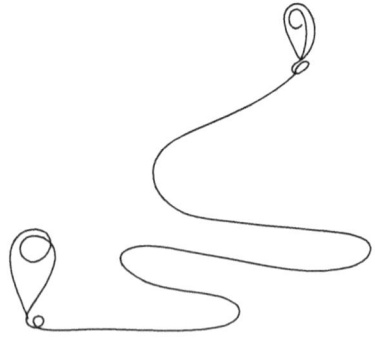

Drakensberg

A tapestry of stars
Above the jagged outline
Of the majestic Drakensberg mountains.
The silence of open spaces,
Where only my breath echoes back to me.

A Myriad of Bubbles

Love is myriads of bubbles,
Varying hues and emotions.
It's a thousand "I love you's,"
Or a single "I hate you."

It is the caress of the warm sun,
The whisper of a cool breeze,
The teasing of the gentle rain.
It is also the raging storm
And crazy winds,
The burning hot or freezing cold.
It's the rain lashing at you
And the darkness that sometimes creeps in.

Love flows through it all,
Not judging, not resisting.
It's buoyant and joyous,
Comforting and reassuring.
Love is defiant and courageous,
Determined and steadfast.
Love does not crumble against the storm,
But rises to ride the waves.

Night Skies

My dad always shines,
Either a sliver of silver
Or a bright shining ball,
With millions more angels flickering around.
There are days when the skies remain dark,
My heart gets a little lost,
But not for long,
For my heart remembers,
The love, and that love carries me through.

Wedding Bells

As the wedding bells chime in the not so distant,
My mind wanders to my dad and my son,
A proud grandfather and a doting little brother.
How joyful we would be
In the celebration of life
If you both chose to stay.

My mind wanders to you every day,
Random specks of memory,
Reminders of love.
Each night, the skies give me a star
To hold me close to the love that once was.

Puzzle

We are all but pieces of the perfect puzzle,
Made to fit, moulding snugly against the next.
Each piece is unique, without replication.
Fit we must, without losing the essence of self.
Therein lies the beauty of this world.

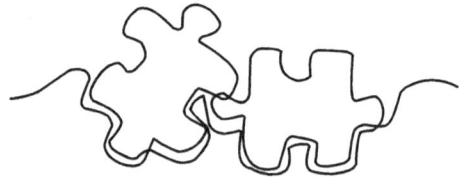

Incomplete

Compete with whom? Why?
I am the sun, and the moon,
The wind and the water,
A bit of all and all in bits.

The sun nourishes my body,
Keeping me warm, helping my growth.
The moon soothes my soul,
Comforting me through dark and light.
The wind caresses my hair and back,
Gently pushing me onwards.
The waters cleanse and quench my thirst.

It seems incomplete,
But I am whole, firmly grounded,
With Mother Earth.

Yes

The eyes smile too,
A fluttering in the heart.
Quick hellos turn into all-night talks.
Can we? Should we?
She asked, and you said yes.
Something the soul and heart
Knew at first glance.

The Clearing

A rocky path lies ahead.
Do not falter or stop; tread carefully.
Do go on, for just up ahead,
Through the clearing is all that you seek.

Is It Too Late?

It is too late, my heart ponders,
To make things right.
Reforestation alongside concrete jungles,
Clean waterways trickling by,
Colourful flowers to bring the bees
And butterflies too.
More grass patches to ground the soul,
Less skies blurred with smog,
To see the night skies in all its glory.
Pristine lengths of sandy beaches,
Oceans lush and thriving.
Is it too late, I wonder,
Will such sights become distant memory soon?

My Current State

I am at a point now
Where I feel like it is a race against time.
There is so much I want to do,
That I didn't do,
That I must still do.
Circumstances, the lack of knowing better,
Responsibilities prevented
Or delayed a great many things.
I am grateful that I am here now.
I wonder if time will ever be enough to
Be all that I can, in this lifetime at least.

Blacksheep

Caged and restrained; unable to just be,
Societal dictates, parental mindsets,
Forced and moulded into the adults we become.

Some learn sooner to break free;
Blacksheep fighting for identity.
Some learn through their children, to break the cycles
Of generations of broken children, broken adults.

Some remain bound in fear, even beyond the grave,
And carry the curses of the ancestors well into the future.
The mind is the master that enslaves the soul.

Gatsheni

Gatsheni, the gentle giant,
A social cohesion quite like humans,
So much more, though,
That man cannot even fathom.
With all our intelligence,
We're often shamed by elephants.
Babies being put through their paces,
Teenagers testing the terrain,
Matriarchs pulling them back into line.
Unruly males, defiant and bullish.
There are lessons of respect,
Of standing your ground,
And of mourning the dead.
A village raising the young, in its truest sense.

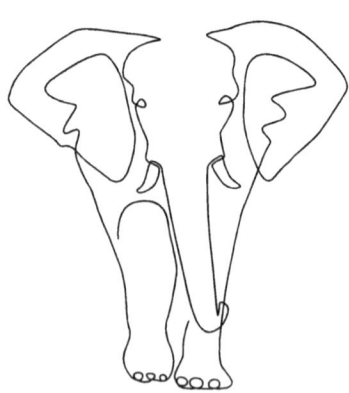

New Me

Of course, I've changed.
Are you not happy?
You don't like the new me.
I've been changing over the years,
You refused to see.
Now, as someone else sees me,
You've stopped to look.

I didn't change for you.
I changed for me.

Cup of Tea

I stand, watching the milk as
It simmers gently on the stovetop.
The kettle whistles, momentarily interrupting
The medley of it all.
The mindless stirring of the tea
To a beautiful hue.
And in that moment, everything is perfect.

Secret Walkway

A walkway so secret,
It draws me in, colours my senses.
Overhead, a canopy, green and lush,
The sun and blue sky streaming in.
Wisps of fragrance fill the air,
Heady and faint, I am led
Further away from the familiar.
A tinkle, a murmur, a childlike giggle.

Is it? Can it be, I wonder?
I hesitate.
Should I go on or turn back?
What if I step into a fairy garden?
What if it is the witch's den?
Going in, I'll find out.
Going back, I'll never know.

Becoming Me

Roots that take up more space,
Branches that offer shade.
Somewhere on this road I travel,
I stopped being needy,
I became needed.
The young ones tell me I'm inspiring.
There was a time I couldn't find inspiration.
It is quite comforting that, in my older years,
I finally became me.

Layers

Peel away the layers,
However many,
You will still only find me.

Paint on the layers,
As many as you wish,
I will still only be me.

A lot of light,
In different hues,
Some bright, some dark.
My layers are many,
But I am only me.

About the Author

Padmini Govender is a poet with a background in financial accounting, but words have always been her true calling. This collection of emotion-evoking and thought-provoking poetry and prose is her first published work. Writing, however, has been woven into her life for as long as she can remember, albeit informally.

Her writing is not always soft and rosy, there are moments of pain that gave rise to many pieces included here, as well as reflective moments contemplating the cruelty and harshness of the world.

Through these pages, there is self-realisation and healing.
In 2022, Padmini joined the Paper Trail Literary Journal group, a supportive community that has been integral to her writing journey. It has provided her with encouragement, feedback, and a sense of belonging, helping her stay focused and inspired through her journey.

Padmini is also an avid photographer with a keen eye for unique perspectives on the mundane and an absolute lover of nature. Her photographs draw the viewer into her world through beautiful imagery, grounding her in the natural world, which is reflected in both her photography and her writing. Some of her photographs have even served as prompts for other poets.

Padmini comes from a long line of resilience. Her great-grandfather arrived in South Africa as an indentured labourer to work on the sugarcane fields of the East Coast. Generations later, she was born as the eldest daughter of a humble plumber and a lively shop clerk. Growing up in Northern KwaZulu-Natal under apartheid, she faced the hardship of being sent to school in another town due to oppressive laws. Yet, even in adversity, she found love and met her husband in that very town. Together, they built a life in a new province at the dawn of democracy, raising two children along the way.

Through the years, Padmini has deepened her connection with the mind, body, spirit, and soul, finding solace and healing in nature. Her poetry is a reflection of this journey, an exploration of struggle, strength, and the quiet beauty of resilience.

www.ingramcontent.com/pod-product-compliance
Lightning Source LLC
Chambersburg PA
CBHW051546010526
44118CB00022B/2594